Fool

KEVIN MILLS

Published by Cinnamon Press
Meirion House,
Glan yr afon,
Tanygrisiau,
Blaenau Ffestiniog,
Gwynedd, LL41 3SU
www.cinnamonpress.com

The right of Kevin Mills to be identified as author of this work has been asserted by him in accordance with the Copyright, Designs and Patent Act, 1988. Copyright © 2009 Kevin Mills.
ISBN: 978-1-905614-80-6

British Library Cataloguing in Publication Data. A CIP record for this book can be obtained from the British Library.

All rights reserved. No part of this publication may be reproduced, stored in a retrieval system, or transmitted in any form or by any means, electronic, mechanical, photocopying, recording or otherwise without the prior written permission of the publishers. This book may not be lent, hired out, resold or otherwise disposed of by way of trade in any form of binding or cover other than that in which it is published, without the prior consent of the publishers.

Designed and typeset in Palatino by Cinnamon Press. Cover design by Mike Fortune-Wood from original artwork 'Fool' by Thane Gorek, used with kind permission.
Printed by the MPG Books Group in the UK
The publisher acknowledges the financial support of the Welsh Books Council

The Biblical quotations are from the NEW AMERICAN STANDARD BIBLE, © 1960, 1962, 1963, 1968, 1971, 1972, 1973, 1975, 1977, 1995 by The Lockman Foundation. Used by permission.
Quotations from the *Mabinogi* are from the translation by Charlotte Guest (1849).

Acknowledgements

Thanks are due to the editors of *Envoi, Planet* and *The New Welsh Review*, in which some of these poems first appeared. I am more indebted than I care to admit to the members of the poetry workshop in Aberystwyth. Diolch yn fawr i chi gyd. Many thanks too to Jan Fortune-Wood and all at Cinnamon Press.

Special thanks, once again, to Alma and Isla.

Biography

Kevin Mills is senior lecturer in English Literature at the University of Glamorgan, where he teaches courses in Shakespeare, Renaissance literature and Mythology. He was born in Caerphilly in 1961. He has published a number of works of literary theory and criticism, the most recent of which *The Prodigal Sign: A Parable of Criticism* is published by Sussex Academic Press (2009). This work combines critical writing with autobiography, dramatic monologues and an aphoristic mode. He has an unpublished novel in a drawer, if anyone's interested.

Contents

am	9
Annunciation	10
Preying	11
Fall	12
Syn	13
Cursive	14
Night-spider	15
Blackspot	16
Break	20
Rev	21
Mine	24
Mission	25
Hommelette	30
Stripping	31
Woodcut	32
Skins	38
Virtual	39
Standing	40
Means	41
Cantrevs	42
1966	54
Manga Boy	55
Outside the Museum of Welsh Life, St Fagans	56
Vale	61
Welsh Lesson	64
Othello, like	65
Fools	66
Stanczyk	71
Insurgence	74

to the memory of Gordon Hughes

Fool

am

In the speech
of gates,

the glottal step
on a pavement,

the raw glimpse
of a song,

the tinnitus
of feathers,

I hear the sun
stammer,

lisp to a white
solstice.

Annunciation

The bell of St Joseph's
seeds the wind;
the green sheets
trimester on the line;

lilac branches prod
the bulge and blossoms
maculate the skin
with sunstain.

Preying

Sun, stand you still on Gibeon;
And you, Moon, in the valley of Ajalon

A blackbird chinks
a quaver of light,
as if noon were mid-
night feathered. As if

the moon's cold fusion
of law and lore
detonated—splitting
the moment—two

cats, identically dark,
stiffen in the hedge.

Fall

Flowers fell and fires
bloomed last autumn
in a valley garden.

On the last day
you raised St John
of the Cross. I

watched the fire wither,
red waves drift
the borders

of the burnt,
the consumed.

Syn

Six is seafood with vinegar;
nine—fried eggs, brown sauce.

I laughed
        (like the smell of cut grass)
when she said.

Her voice like blackberries,
marimba eyes.

Cursive

Hexing the pane, pluvial stars abra-
cadabraed finite angles, banished
from one infinite circle. The
wet spell kept us indoors,
by fire's sympathy with
glass. A wandlight at
the curtain edge
disappeared
like this
word

Night-spider

A place's unlacing
draws in the horizon.

A wire through
the overgrowth skitters

like nerve. A dry vein
in the epidermis beats

its nocturne on a string.
A track through bracken

winds a gossamer shudder.
Somewhere near—hangs

                by a thread.

Blackspot

1

Snow flying under tarmac,
blue stars rising from black
ground. Gravity shoving
up the roof.

A cloud exhales
condensed bone; darkness
breaking out through
woven glass.

2

This is a dead man's
car. It's doubled
the clock when I get
behind the wheel.

Don't diesels run
forever? My miles follow
his as if I were the ghost
in his machine.

3

Blow into the tube.
The chip reckons
I'm innocent.

I think of his last
breath and imagine
a cosmic beep.

4

I shelter at 93.4
kilohertz, waving

down white
noise. *Shh* the starsnow
says between stations.
RDS fails to keep me

tuned in transit.
Frequencies drift
through the hiss
of scattered codes.

Stop at the lights.
Retune.

Break

Stop off in Lland-
overy, near Llewelyn
ap Gruffydd's armour,

vacated
on the castle mound.
Read the plaque

explaining the ruin
and turn back.
On the passenger seat

there's a new translation
of *Gilgamesh*. I think
about respraying.

Rev

In 1927, Parry Thomas was killed while attempting the land speed record at Pendine (Carmarthenshire). In 1969, Owen Wyn-Owen dug up and restored his car.

1969

Clutched from slow
sand, a car's rev-
enant rounded the
vertical bend, throttled

in chain. Towed
out of the subsoil's
lay-by, skin wealed,
and buckled,

innards eaten by forty-two
years of salt. To Wyn-
Owen the car-
case was a task.

2007

Turning over
the ridge, spokes of a wind-
farm slip through Roman
numerals. Close faux-Cor-

busier space finds time
for idle engines. The ghost
of Parry's machine bleeds
on the chequered floor.

Built for such a haunt-
ing—Museum of Speed—
lined with mono-
chrome stills.

1927

On the low tide's part-
time highway, midday
gathered watchers, cran-
ing into turbu-

lence, to read the measured
mile. Lindsay-Lloyd,
the RAC men, Dunlop,
Shell and locals, press

and newsreel hacks clocked
the final run—there, they
must have thought, to judge
the quick.

Mine

to Jeff Hankins

Huge player in the back
of the Beetle, bend-

ing *The Circle
Game*. Joni mining

our mood. Coming down
into Merthyr from Dow-

lais top, rain slagging
off open-cast November

roads. You would hunch,
the wheel under your chin,

lean into being aim-
less as the screening

water. An occluded front
opened stars over Carn Bugail.

Today I slide in the CD,
my V-dub crooning the

A468. Cars like painted ponies
on the Tesco roundabout.

Mission

in memory of my Mother

1. Leda in the Cambrians

She rode the hill at eve-
ning shadowed by a man who died
of exposure—his white hand

hooked on stiffening air.
She knew him from chap-
el. He sang the words wrong

and scratched slub with long nails.
His cold skin stretched over
roots, frost feathering

the torso. That field where,
spooking the whole sky, kites
carry blood to the sun.

2. Bridging

It was when the drip-
ping man in the High
Street pointed to the bridge
not taken, and

said: *bid me come
unto thee upon the waters,*

that she reflected on
the incomprehensibility
of bridges and the dryness
of the sane.

3. Prayer Meeting

She tried to conjure a prayer
for Miss Hughes and the hill
tribes, their teeth black
with beetel nuts and idolatry.

Paint scrolled from cold
edges that refused the white,
huffing it into blisters.
The electric bar

cracked the damp, timbers
squealed dissent. Black capillaries
sucked rheum into the walls
from the dark acre.

4. Deputation

They wanted to know about Baalbek—
how Jesus played with the Ishmaelites.
She spoke of the pains of learning

Arabic and of the gap. They made
her a sandwich and dropped her
off near the Cock and Bull,

drove home discussing the Muslim.
An angel took her to Lime Street,
trains to Builth Road.

5. Leaving Newbridge

on Wye, my mother's child-
hood home, going south

the road elbows me
left to a red

light. When track met
track at this low junc-

tion, she lit out
for Beirut.

Idling on the bridge,
the engine dreams

of dual carriage-
way, from Merthyr

Tydfil to Cardiff. A quarter
mile back are unmarked

graves in a dead church-
yard. A few desultory

spots. Not enough
for wipers.

Amber
now.

Hommelette

He said
the trinity
was an egg.

My father never
came out
of his shell,

but I sensed
the infinite border
he concealed.

Stripping

I found an orange
in the back pages of my bed-
room wall, a rose-
bud parchment, a leaf-blown

glypta. In all the annals
of earlier possession,
the ghosts of wiped-down
mould trace faint caesurae.

Woodcut

1. Advice

Without a vice, the perfect
cut slips the saw's
grasp, the drill equivocates.

Here's a scar ingrained —
a rough track
for the fallen
angle.

2. Measure

Millimetres crawl
on jointless legs away
from any mark.
They have no

nest. They feed on raw
anxiety and slivers
of dead time.

3. Glue

is a matter of hope.
You sweat out the drying
and feel nervously

for play. At school
they taught us dove-
tailing. Nothing
stuck.

4. Filler

is redemption tubed.
It lies for you

between
intent and action,
mind and (slipping) world.

5. Spirit Level

It all rests squarely
on this:
a trapped

bubble:
a little zero
dividing the equals.

6. Offcuts

Among the accidental
objects shaved
and stripped
from shelving—

a blond ringlet of dust,
       curled from the bit,
   cutting implausible
          form.

Skins

1
I wrote this on a rizla—
between you and me. I lick-
ed the edge, stuck it in Bert-
rand Russell. Tomorrow I'
ll find Occam again.

2
Venetian stripes canal-
ising light. I used to think
this would be the cover
of my first album. Is there
water? Just my blinds.

3
Smoke, too, I imagine.
Enough of it stuck to keep
me sucking in self-imm-
olation, and blowing out
what unskeined illusion?

4
That white Egyptian
cotton shirt. You liked it
so much you wanted me
to take it off. Red wine
wasn't it? In the end?

5
I wrote this on a rizla—
blue pack. Fine. Pencil
sharpened to philosoph-
ical nicety. And still half
a line left.

Virtual

Static held to
my screen two crossed
hairs, as I fired
off to you an e-bullet-
in.
      Had we met,
say next Friday,
all but silent on the
subject of dates,
      would you
have seen the scope
for prohibited
domains, erased
by that last symbol—

x ?

Standing

to Damian Walford Davies

11-ish, I think, lining up
for the hole in the wall.
I'll look for you. We'll
talk—recall the time.

You'll tell me of lost al-
ignments—overlooked
repetitions, unheard rhythms
of I and I. Italic shadow

quotes my slight lean. There
you'll be in cool sil-
houette—the light field all
about you. 11.10, maybe. 11.11.

Means

Flemish masons curved
stone across the valley,
cutting air with cunei
while miners glo-
wed in the underworld.

The viaduct ponders
with a long mm
the young body falling
through an untranslatable
cartouche.

Cantrevs

– relating to the Mabinogion –

Prologue: four branches

i
I have never seen a tree
half on fire from root
to crown,

but green tongues stem
from acute axils.

ii
My mother a garrulous
monoglot; my father
fluent but dumb.

My nieces and nephews
sprang from the sibilant
litter of flames and leaves.

iii
He burned the clippings
late in the day, the sky
ripening in Percy's Field.

Green smoke. Too much
sap for flame. Black
umbilicus in the shadow

of the coalhouse. Was there
a hawthorn?

iv
Outside my gate, four
branches of the plane
tree connect

with phone lines. I
recall his voice
as the smell of
pine.

1. Rhiannon

It will avail nothing for anyone
to follow yonder lady.

Redheaded tele-
path. I never saw
the horse she said she
rode to nowhere

over hurdles in a Flint-
shire field.

We spoke
                remotely
for three months.

I knew I only
had to ask,
after I'd asked.

2. Pryderi

behold a claw came through the window...
And at the door behold there was an infant boy

The night you were born I
fell, my foot clawed
under the bike. Wet road,
pothole. Twenty-two years
passed. Yesterday I twist-

ed my ankle on the stairs,
and I thought
of a rainy night—anxiety
broken down to one
umbilicate depression.

3. Bendigeidfran

The head will be to you as pleasant company
as it ever was

The rooks and daws that bless
my roof, with black
zest fend off pigeons.
What enters

his head as he turns
in at the gate is
the compass of its territory —
blue turf and scope, edge

unfound. But in the flap
and caw, you'd think it
fenced by incantatory
barbing of the air.

4. Arianrhod

He shall never have a name until he receives one from me

My mother kept a bird-
book on the folding
table near the window,
to find their names. She called
me by her dead brother's
name, by my dead
father's name—the brain's
little binoculars
unable to pick me out.

She pointed to
troglodytes troglodytes
on a pine-branch, needles
threading light.

5. Blodeuwedd

We will seek... by charms and illusion,
to form a wife... out of flowers

Meadowsweet, oak, and broom
make her smile,
a creamware vase on the sill.

Histamines flock
in my sinuses,
nettle my eyes.

One night, an owl,
eyes like white poppies,
turned her head.

6. Manawydan

Let us go into Lloegr, and seek
some craft

I worked in England seven years—
Worcester, Oxford, Portsmouth.

Beyond the bridge Gwent
was invisible, seafog

cursing the daylight
levels, rain thick as sack.

Loose coins for the bin
uneasy on the passenger seat.

Scrape together.
Exact change.

7. Rhonabwy

No one knows the dream…
because of the various colours

It is hard to tell
why the green laurels
in the white light
in the night's drizzle
dream you up.

Yet there you are
on the wall's edge
where Broom Hill gives
onto Flint Street,
a pebble in your palm.

Your brother says
you remember me.

8. Olwen

*She comes here every Saturday
to wash her head*

You were washing your hair
when the white trail
of foam escaped your

fingers, to blaze down
between the ridges
of your spine.

I followed its diminishing
path. You said I was
impossible.

*

Grass, beaten
white, trailed from the road
to the cup-marked megalith.

You stood on the stone's corpse
and said you could see the way
from Llancaiach to Nelson—

the long downhill to the junc-
tion, picked clean by streetlights.

9. Heilyn

*So he opened the door and looked
towards Cornwall*

The west-facing door
stuck in winter, unseasoned
stiles forced against jambs.

Spring unsealed it. Late
March, my brother knocked.
We each saw dad

fleetingly on the thresh-
hold. How long
was it?

10. Goewin

He made Goewin…

There is a bench, moatside,
where two Caer-
phillys fumble. One feels
the ardent easterlies
bunching its silk
against the walls.

Captured Nant-Y-
Gledyr bends to accommo-
date the coupling.
Below the water, the darker
town imagines itself
uppermost.

1966

Wet sheets
evaporate to bone, blankets
buckle. He's taken to the back
room to see the buckets
tip spoil over Bed-

was. Eyes closed, they move
in his head. A black vein
trips their beat. If
they would stop. Rain
folds the glass and ripples

until the whole slides
in water. He's carried back
for another shift in the sick-
room. Slowly the thing
subsides.

Manga Boy

for Josh

Little anime in flesh,
eyes lacquered by the telly,
sitting close up to the screen
so no light escapes him.

The good news, he says,
is that he's going to Japan;
the bad news—he hates fish.

He's back among the great-eyed
kids at war with techno-demons,
and we are lost in the floating
room behind him.

Outside the Museum of Welsh Life, St Fagans

for Howard

1

We picked among museum pieces
assembled from some other Wales.
Rebuilt in consumer space,
in reasonable time
—the structures that enclosed the hours—
sheepfold, church, mill and home.

We came here to see how far a longhouse stretches,
to duck through doorways
fitted to smaller lives than ours.
Stone and timber history reminds us
we have outgrown it,
becoming incommensurable.

2

This building, this one,
was once in the Elan Valley.

Long division of stone,
of lintel, slate and beam,
coding of detritus,
translation into diagram—
plotted this reunion
of unbuilt integers.

The mathematics of identity
has drawn us here.

3

My mother used to say she'd been a guest
in these four walls before they were unlaced.
But now her bones unlace and she is missed,
where the house once stood—now open space.

4

No-one needs a jug now.
Not the kind of thing you buy.
Blue and white, it once held milk.
It stood on a white tablecloth,

laid out for forgotten teatime,
with bone-handled knives,
jamspoons, butter dishes,
cups and saucers, matching plates.

These things were getting old
when I was young. This setpiece
is the 1950s, intact, consumable,
approximating history.

I like the prefab best.

5

BBC Wales—
documentary on St Fagans,
the science of moving buildings
out of redundancy into history.
I remembered being there:
the technique of a daytrip—
turning friendship
into shared history.

Outside the museum,
we looked at the queue for the A4232
and suddenly felt aggrieved.

Vale

Running Away with the Hairdresser by Kevin Sinnott
National Museum of Wales

1

I carn run in these bloody 'eels,
I said, an' then I seen Barry.
'E was comin' out
a the Stairtion, lookin' a' me. Arf
cut, wa'n 'e. Bu' love 'im
'is shirt was angin' out
an' 'e looked like shit. In fact
'e looked like looking like
shit was 'is ambition. An' I
thought—*I carn do
it to 'im mun.*

Drippy bastard.
My 'and slipped from Torny's a
mo, an' I was thinking'—*Christ
I 'aven got no cloes
nor nothin'*, and Barry's shit-
faced an' thass Roj on the sill
an' Debbie's' 'ad the bairby
an' everythin', an' I thought—
na. Fuck'em. I thought—*fuck 'em.
Fuck'em all. I'm off, inni.*

2

Aw, look a' me mun. My 'air
da look mad, an' my skirt's all
crumpled. My legs
are nice though, in they?
      Torny's jus done my 'air
by there. 'E was ticklin' me with 'is
brush an' sayin' I was gorjus.

'E thinks iss bollocks
cos we're big, like,
an' the buildin's are all
small. *We're clorss,*
I said, *an' the buildin's are farther
away.* Bu' 'e da look so
ugly. Thass why 'e dorn like i'

3

See my 'and. Well, iss incredible
right. My 'and is right
by the window where we
done it. Tha' was the room, like.
'Oness t'God, now. I' was tha'
very room.
        An' see the telegraph pole?
Looks like iss stuck to my arse? Well
i' da lean like tha' in real life. Bu'
the lampors in front of Torny, tha
curvy white one, that da make i' look
a bit like 'e's wankin'? Thass
no' there at all mun.

        I da think the road is pink
and blue, see, and iss a bit like we're
runnin' in the sky. No' really, like.
I da jus say tha'.

Welsh Lesson

I been to the cassle, I 'ave,
'cos I was gerrin' on my mother's
nerves. Gorra phorto a me
by the tower tha' da
lean orver like iss fallin'.
     'E was mad. Spork
Welsh 'e did, an' 'e tried
ta teach us. Bu' we was rubbish.
Couldn' do the souns, like. Iss
cass-tell irris. You gorra say ll
on the end. Bit like you was larfin'
to yourself.
     An' iss not *Car*-philly; iss
Caer-ffili, an' you da' say the *rr*
inni. After tha' we called 'im
Rothy, 'cos when there's two
d's, you say *th*, like.
     Dunno whar 'appened
to 'im. My mother wouldn' say
nothin'. Burr I thought I seen
'im once in Cardiff. (*Caer-deethe*,
you da say). 'E was with someone
else, an' she ad' sunglasses
on an i' was rainin'.
     'E wa'n lookin'.
     I never said nothin'.

Othello, like

I da like Shairkspeare. Done
'im in school, we did. Wass tha'
one now where 'e da strangle 'er?
She 'adden done nothin', like,
but 'e da think she been shaggin'
'is mairt.

Bit depressin' mind. They're
rareciss, they are, and they didn'
like 'im cos 'e was black. My fren's
Airzhun, and they da call 'er Paki,
an' she da say they can piss off.
She's a nutter mun.

My dad da call 'er blondie.
'E thinks iss funny, like, cos she's
no' really blond. She gor assma.
She da carry one of them things
with 'er. Carn always breathe
proper, see.

Fools

Fools because of their transgression... are afflicted (Ps. 107:17).

1. Mess

Look at that clown in the temple,
clattering the tables, coins
jumping through the holy
of holies.
         See him tripping
over thin-legged lambs, splat-
tered by the patina of panicked
doves, his whip of knotty string
a crazy pennant over the tabernacle.

They'll paint him
red and blue.

2. Rider Deck Fool

Is he surfing? The impossible
promontory a cobbled board
on the rip of those blue hills?

Or is it the world's edge
under that camp boot—the colour
of the yellow sky?

What does the white dog know,
pawing the imp-
ending air?

3. Pierrot

Beyond the gate of heaven
he hung
around, the iridescent play
amusing his skin.

In a suit of impossible snow—
his everyday
best—he took the sin of boyhood
for a game.

The label against his heart
said *cool iron*,
so they manacled him to the
outside.

4. Punch

Hangman Jack swag-
gering his noose, the baby
slipping into widening jaws,

he shrugs, clacks
his stick on wooden flesh,
steals the bangers,
swazzling his contempt.

The plod wants to cuff
him, but who else can say—
I've killed the devil?

5. Del Boy

Knocked-off
tat and fenced-out white
goods crammed in
the wannabe penthouse.

Behind that gewgaw bar,
are there tools of trade?
Suitcase, jemmy, blade,
hobbling post?

He pulls a King Edward
from the biscuit
barrel and grins,
already a millionaire

in the stolen currency
of dreams.
              One day
they'll nail him.

Stanczyk

1. Just

So there's this bear,
shipped for the hunt,
roaring from the east,
bombing through our
positions, blazing
eyes, arms flying. His
Maj is screaming

Shoot the fucking bear!
Shitting himself.
I'm thinking
Can bears climb trees?
Some lackey lands
an arrow in its maw
and off it goes to bleed.

Now he's coming at me
from behind the
bush, like it's my fault.
*Who put the bloody
beast in the green
zone, anyway? I say. No
place for bears.*

2. Miscarriage

There was blood on her
skirts. I could tell
two kinds of agony in one
face when she clutched

at the draining belly,
leaking life into the mush-
roomed ground. Aborted
pleasure, the game soured,

quacks fannying in chambers
with stiff linen and clun-
king bowls, leeches
dripping like fresh-culled kid-

neys, along stained corridors.
I know my fault, your majesty,
but it doesn't bleed in a tin
bucket. It rules me.

3. Party

What does it take to end
a party?
They dance a phalanx,

charade
the works of poets, philosophers,
swallow

slivovitz, tales of war, satire,
cirrhotic
organon thickening heads.

And some-
where bodies are burning for want
of metaphors.

Think too little you're a clown,
too much
you're an egghead. I have

a few
lines left. Too few to

Insurgence

1

From under the cabinet
they drive out—
a small convoy of dark
armour over the sandy
laminate. The telly's on.

News 24.
Yesterday's sweep
picked off the slow,
the overturned—crawling
dust bagged (with crum-

bled food, skinflakes,
hairs) and binned. Today,
as I watch them range,
the window shudders
at a drill in Bethel Close.

2

The one-time occupants of unsealed
borders, brown bodied, substantial,
have gone. In their place pale,
thin, arachnid spooks hook them-
selves on sparse weft.

The trick is to appear un-spidered,
to attenuate the phobic twitch
that brings down boot or news-
print on an unarmed thorax. Not much
of a predator, you'd think,

this weightless knot in cross-
ed threads, but certain lights catch
woven corners where all the air
reticulates, every space closed
between walls, objects, white goods.

3

How did that dark spat-
tering find a home?

                    The kind
of life that clings to walls

as if a shadow left a stain,
arrives hooded in moisture,

crossing
thresholds

by the subterfuge of blind
nonentity.

Ineradicable, its roots
are the capillaries that open

every wall. It feeds on
the hand that bites it,

mapping its territory
with its own thin body.